sara bareilles
KALEIDOSCOPE HEART

MW00582105

This book was approved by Sara Bareilles

Piano/vocal arrangements by John Nicholas

Cherry Lane Music Company
Director of Publications/Project Editor: Mark Phillips
Manager of Publications: Rebecca Skidmore

ISBN: 978-1-60378-290-6

Visit our website at www.cherrylaneprint.com

sara bareilles
KALEIDOSCOPE HEART

Hi.

It's me, Sara. As I've said before, I don't do those fancy bios. So sue me.

Kaleidoscope Heart is my new album, and I'm beyond proud of this collection of songs, in no small part due to the fact it was like pulling teeth to write them.

We spent the better part of three years touring and supporting my first record, *Little Voice,* and by the end of that process I was completely burnt out. Don't get me wrong; it was an unbelievable ride that far surpassed my expectations in the best way. We had some unforgettable high points as well as some very humbling low ones, and like any good roller coaster, it's exhilarating but you still feel a little bit sick at the end and are happy to have your feet on the ground again.

I thought that I would use our much-needed time off to just pour myself into writing, but I actually found that I wanted nothing to do with music for a little while. I preferred drinking copious amounts of coffee, going to yoga, and looking for cute throw pillows at Target. I love throw pillows.

As the time passed, I slowly started writing again, and truly amazed myself with just how horrible the songs were. And then the fear set in.

I think I fell victim to what a lot of artists go through with a second record: the expectations, the pressure, the anxiety of what's to come, the idea that maybe I've already written my best work...

Weeks before I was supposed to start recording, I was in full-scale panic-attack mode, feeling pressure to start the ball rolling again, but not having material I cared about. I only had about four new songs that I really loved, and the rest were truly embarrassing. Thankfully, over a margarita, my good friend Matt said something profound and poetic that made it all come clear:

He said, "You can't polish a turd. A bad song is a bad song. Ask for more time."

And so I did.

My manager suggested only recording the four songs I loved and I agreed. Thank God he did, because the floodgates opened after a taste of what being in the studio would look and feel like. It was easy, and exciting, and infinitely inspiring. I wrote the rest of the record in about a month, largely based around the song "Uncharted" that still feels like the centerpiece to me. My fear of what was to come was keeping me from doing anything. And finally, I cared about what I was saying.

As homage to the song that freed me, I took the title of the record from its lyrics.

My counterpart in the studio, Neal Avron, is one of my Buddhas in this world. He's one of the most patient, musical, kind, and dedicated people I've ever met. We were an odd pairing for sure, as he's best known for his rock records (Fall Out Boy, Say Anything), and I do covers of songs from *Dumbo* and love *The Golden Girls*. But it was exciting and felt completely right. We spent about six months making this record, and the record that came from it is exactly what I wanted. With Neal's help, I took risks, and pushed myself both as a player and vocally, and I followed my gut wholeheartedly for the very first time. And I can't wait to share it.

I can't wait to see these songs come to life. I can't wait to reconnect with fans from the stage. I can't wait to see how many times the word *kaleidoscope* gets misspelled.

I can't wait to get on the ride again.

CONTENTS

Hearts have col - ors, don't we all know.

Hearts have col - ors, don't we all know.

Red runs through our veins.

Red runs through our veins.

Feel _____ the fi - re burn - ing up. _____ In - spi - re me _____ with

(Feel _____ the fi - re burn - ing up. _____ In - spi - re me _____ with

Ooh,

ah. _____

5

blood   of   blue _____ and   green.
blood   of   blue _____ and   green.)

I   have   hope. _____   In - side   is   not   a   heart, _

I   have   hope. _____   In - side   is   not   a   heart, _

but   a   ka - lei - do - scope.

but   a   ka - lei - do - scope.

Uncharted

Words and Music by
Sara Bareilles

no bro-ken heart, __ no fa-mil-iar scars. __ This ter-ri-to-ry

goes un - chart-ed. __

Just me __ in a room sunk down in a house in a town, and I

don't breathe, __ though I nev-er meant to let it get a-way from me. __ Now I've

D.S. al Coda I

11

Coda I

G7   *Am*

Ab7   *Bbm*

ed. It's all ___ un - chart - ed. Jump - start my ka -

E/G#   *G*   *D*

F/A   *Ab*   *Eb*

lei - do - scope heart. I love to watch the col - ors fade. ___ They may not ___

F   *E7*   *Am*

Gb   *F7*   *Bbm*

___ make sense, but they sure as hell made ___ me. I won't go as a

E/G#   *G*   *D*

F/A   *Ab*   *Eb*

pas - sen - ger, no, ___ wait - ing for the road to ___ be ___ laid. Though I may ___

be go-ing down, ___ I'll take in flame ___ o-ver burn-ing out. ___

Com-pare where you are to where you want to be, and you'll get

D.S. al Coda II

Coda II

no-where. I'm go-

La, la, la, ___ ah. ___

Gonna Get Over You

Words and Music by
Sara Bareilles and Sam Farrar

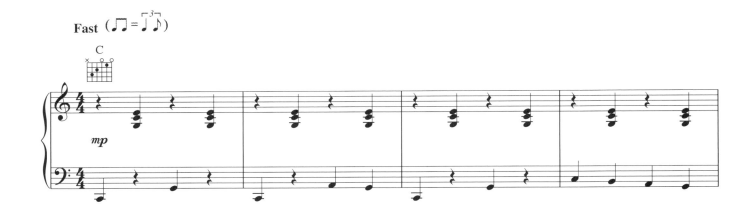

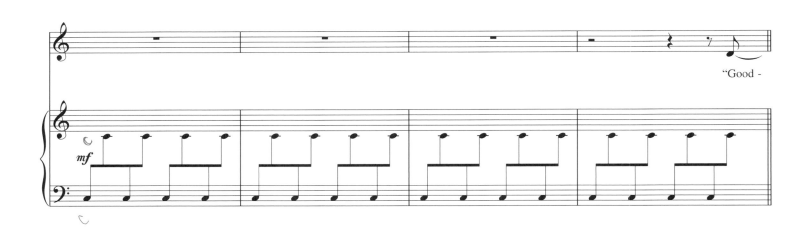

14

18

D.S. al Coda I

Coda I

once I find ___ the ___ oth - er side ___ of ___ some - day. ___

Oh, ___ oh, woh, ___

oh, oh, ___

oh, woh, ___ ooh, ___ woh. ___

22

Hold My Heart

Words and Music by
Sara Bareilles

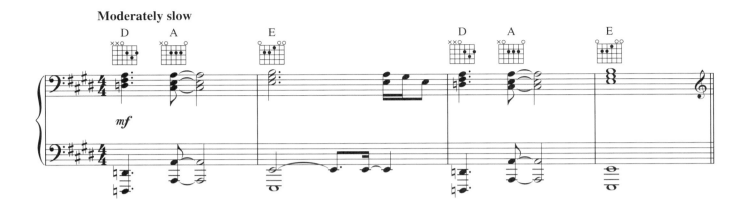

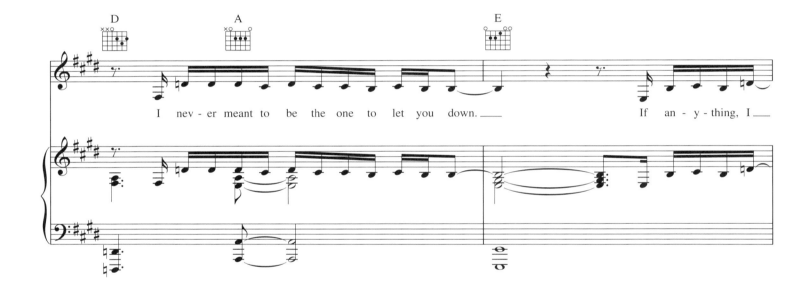

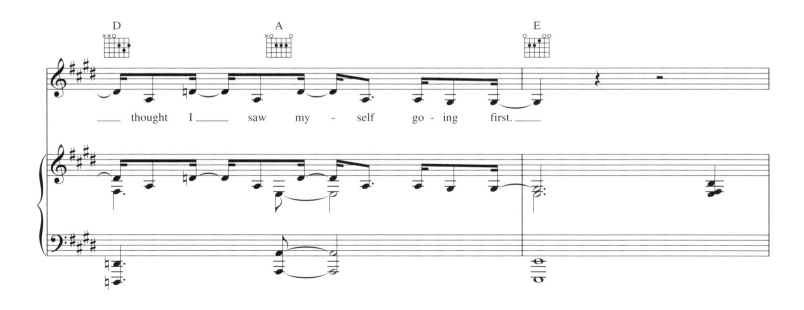

I did-n't want to tell you you were right, _____ like the sea-

son chang-ing; __ oh, __ I __ felt it, too. _____ Does

an-y-bod-y know _____ how to hold __ my heart, how to hold __

__ my heart, __ 'cause I don't want to let __ go, let go, let go __ too __ soon. I

want to tell you so _____ be - fore the sun ___ goes ___ dark, ___ how to hold _

___ my heart, ____ 'cause I don't want to let ____ go, let go, let go ___ of ___ you. ___

To Codas I & II

King of Anything

Words and Music by
Sara Bareilles

a - gree? You are not ___ me. Who made you King ___ of An - y - thing? So

you dare ___ tell me who to be? ___ Who died ___ and made you King ___

___ of An - y - thing? ___ Oh, ___ who cares ___ if you dis - a - gree? ___ You are not ___

___ me. Who made you King ___ of An - y - thing? So you dare ___ tell me who

Say You're Sorry

Words and Music by
Sara Bareilles

Pa - per cut ti - gers start - ing to bleed. __
Now I don't need __ it, at least not with you. __

Hang from your tight - rope a - bove all the mess, __
So if you see __ him, the man 'neath the mask, __

and just say __ you're sor - ry, no more, no less. __
tell him __ I'm leav - ing and not look - ing back. __

Words you ___ won't ___ use, you don't ___ feel them
Words are ___ no ___ use; you don't ___ need them

like ___ I do. _____ (I do, ___ I do.) _____
like ___ I do, _____ ooh. _____

Show will ___ be o - ver soon. _____ It's not the

cur - tain clos - ing caus - ing us to call it a day. _____ I want to walk a - way _____

45

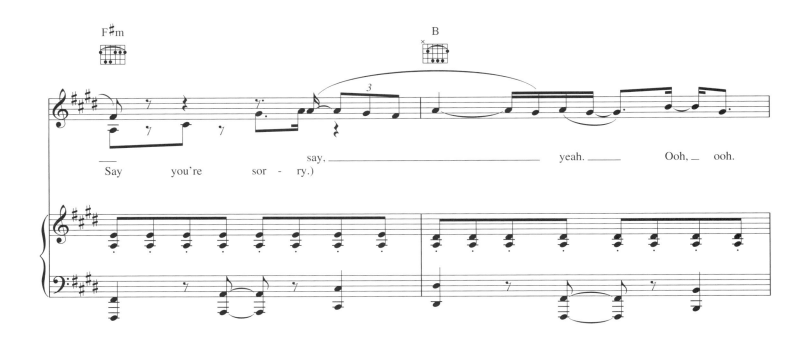

F#m ⬚⬚⬚   B ⬚⬚⬚

say, _____ yeah. _____ Ooh, _ ooh.
Say you're sor - ry.)

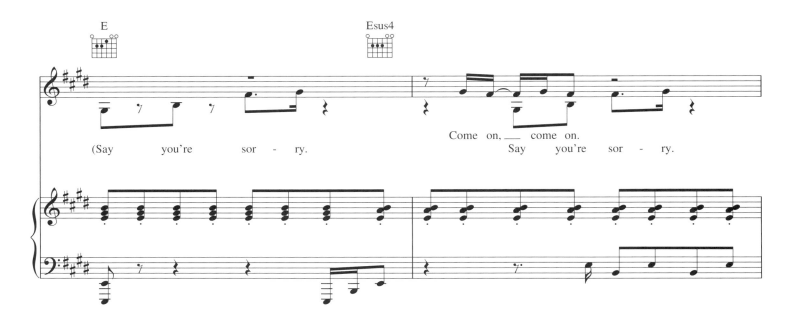

E ⬚⬚⬚   Esus4 ⬚⬚⬚

Come on, ___ come on.
(Say you're sor - ry.   Say you're sor - ry.

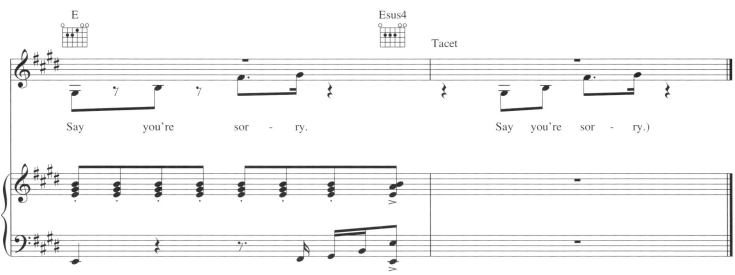

E ⬚⬚⬚   Esus4 ⬚⬚⬚   Tacet

Say you're sor - ry.   Say you're sor - ry.)

46

The Light

Words and Music by
Sara Bareilles

Fast

In the morn - ing it comes; ___ heav - en sent a hur - ri - cane.

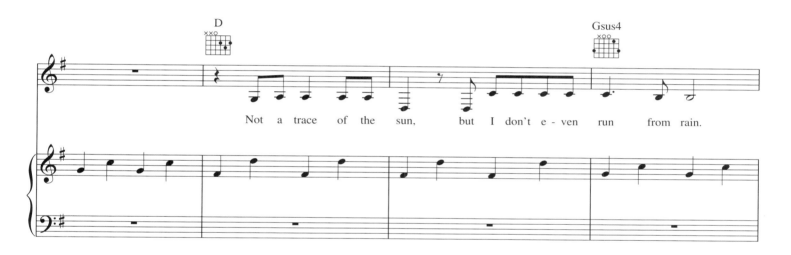

Not a trace of the sun, but I don't e - ven run from rain.

Beat - ing out of my chest, my heart is hold - ing on to you,

from the mo - ment I __ knew, from the mo - ment I __ knew.

You're the air in my breath, fill - ing up my

love - soaked lungs. Such a beau - ti - ful mess, __

__ in - ter - twined __ and o - ver - run. __

*On *D.S.*, play R.H. an octave lower.

trust you, babe, gon-na look in your eyes.

And if you say we'll be all right,

I'll fol-low you

in-to the light.

50

is right here __ be - side ____ me. ___

I'm not e - nough, I ___ swear it, ___ but take my

love ____ and ___ wear it o - ver ____ your

shoul - ders. ____ And if you ___ say ___

we'll be all right, _____ I'm gon - na _____ _____ trust you, _____ babe, _____ gon - na look in _____ your ___ eyes. ___

And if you _____ say _____ we'll be all right, _____

Basket Case

Words and Music by
Sara Bareilles

*Guitarists: Use open-D tuning (low to high): D-A-D-F♯-A-D.

steady hand and I got used to it.
steel train touch and I'm just a track you lay.

And a
So I'll

glass cage heart and invited me in,
stay right here underneath you.

and now I'm just a basket case without him.
I'm just a basket case and that's what we do.

You're begging for the

58

bas - ket ____ case. _____ I

2.

Won't __ some-bod - y _____ come on in _____ and

tug at my seams. __ Oh, send _____ your __ ar - mies in _____ of

rob - bers and thieves __ to steal _____ the _____ state I'm in. I don't ____

Let the Rain

Words and Music by
Sara Bareilles

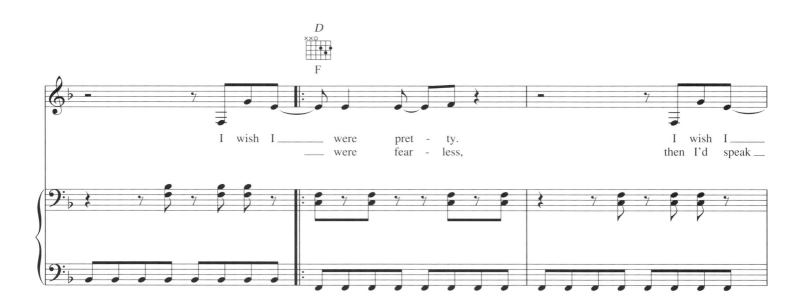

I wish I _____ were pret - ty.
_____ were fear - less,

I wish I _____
then I'd speak __

_____ were   brave. _____
_____ my   truth, _____

If I   owned _____ this   cit - - y,
and the   world _____ would   hear _ this.

1.

then   I'd   make _____ it   be - have. _____   And if I _____
That's   what   I _____

2.

_____ wish   I'd _____ do,   yeah, _____

Now who shouts at the top of her voice?__ Let me go.__ Let me out. This is not__ my choice.__ And I al - ways felt it be - fore__ that the world__ was filled with much more__ than the drown - ing soul I've learned to be.__ I just need the rain to re - mind__ me. I want to

D.S. al Coda

68

Machine Gun

Words and Music by
Sara Bareilles

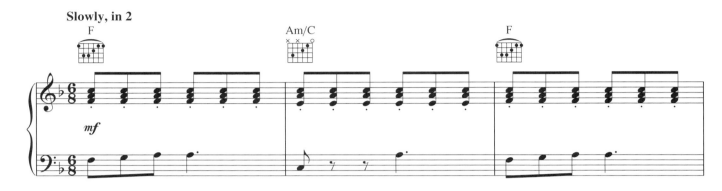

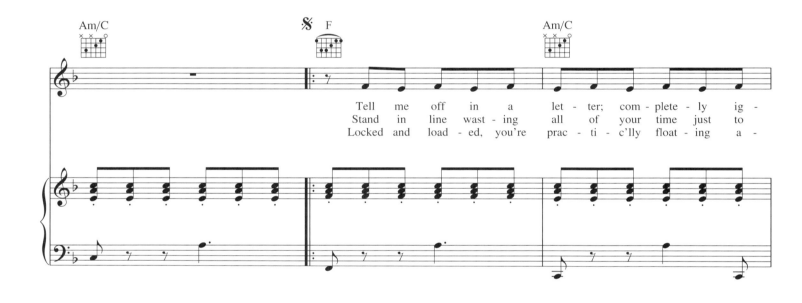

Tell me off in a letter; com - plete - ly ig -
Stand in line wast - ing all of your time just to
Locked and load - ed, you're prac - ti - c'lly float - ing a -

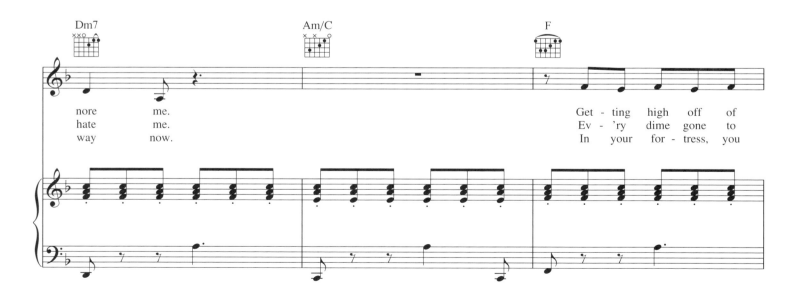

nore me.
hate me.
way now.

Get - ting high off of
Ev - 'ry dime gone to
In your for - tress, you

say - ing why you don't a - dore me.
ways you can find that might bait me
feel like you're more or less safe now.

and Ba - by, please. ___
But let me say, ___ I

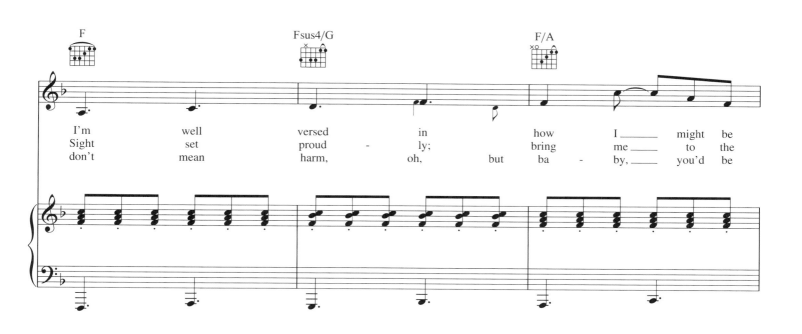

I'm well versed in how I ___ might be
Sight set proud - ly; bring me ___ to the
don't mean harm, oh, but ba - by, ___ you'd be

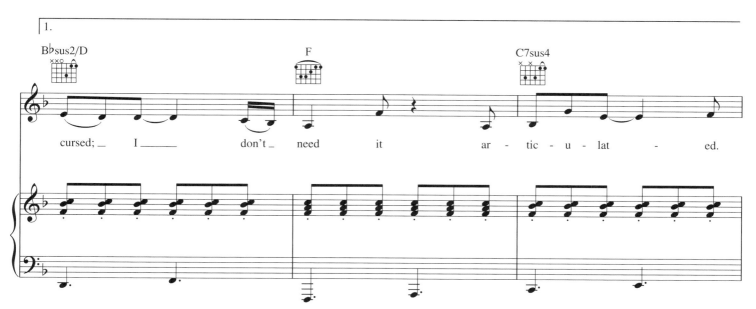

1.

cursed; ___ I ___ don't ___ need it ar - tic - u - lat - ed.

Don't just hide in the si-lence be-hind what you've real-ly been try'n' to say. ____ Yeah, ____ yeah. ____

What a skill, ba-by, aim-ing to kill me with words you _____ don't

Not Alone

Words and Music by
Sara Bareilles

the mon-sters aren't real. You're mak-ing me

feel I'm not a - lone.

(Woo, hoo.) I'm not a - lone.

Ooh. (Woo, hoo.)

84

Breathe Again

Words and Music by
Sara Bareilles

85

Bluebird

Words and Music by
Sara Bareilles

Word came through _____ in a let - ter,

one of us _____ chang - ing our _____ minds. _____   You won't

More Great Piano/Vocal Books
FROM CHERRY LANE

For a complete listing of Cherry Lane titles available,
including contents listings, please visit our web site at
www.cherrylane.com

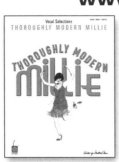

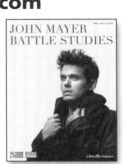
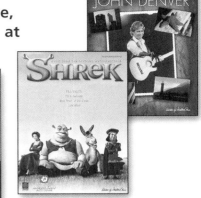

See your local music dealer or contact:

7777 W. BLUEMOUND RD. P.O. BOX 13819 MILWAUKEE, WI 53213

Prices, contents and availability subject to change without notice.

0310